She Loved Baseball
THE EFFA MANLEY STORY

WRITTEN BY
Audrey Vernick

ILLUSTRATED BY
Don Tate

Collins
An Imprint of HarperCollins Publishers

Collins is an imprint of HarperCollins Publishers

She Loved Baseball: The Effa Manley Story

Text copyright © 2010 by Audrey Vernick Illustrations copyright © 2010 by Don Tate
All rights reserved. Manufactured in China. No part of this book may be used or reproduced
in any manner whatsoever without written permission except in the case of brief quotations
embodied in critical articles and reviews. For information address HarperCollins Children's Books,
a division of HarperCollins Publishers, 195 Broadway, New York, NY 10007.
www.harpercollinschildrens.com

Library of Congress Cataloging-in-Publication Data
Vernick, Audrey.
  She loved baseball : the Effa Manley story / written by Audrey Vernick, illustrated by Don Tate.
   p. cm.
  ISBN 978-0-06-134920-1 (trade bdg.)
  1. Manley, Effa, 1897–1981. 2. Women baseball team owners—United States—Biography.
3. African American women—United States—Biography. 4. Newark Eagles (Baseball team)—
History. 5. African American business enterprises—New Jersey—Newark. I. Title.
GV865.M325V47 2010   2009035010
796.357092—dc22   CIP
[B]   AC

Typography by Sarah Hoy
20 SCP 11
❖
First Edition

For two fine baseball-loving men, Jules Glassman, my
father, and Michael Vernick, my husband, all-stars both
—A.V.

For five extraordinary women who changed my life:
Tamera D.-T., Sharon T., Dorothy B., Autumn S., Jheris T.
—D.T.

When she was in first grade, Effa Brooks was called to the principal's office.

"Young lady," the principal said, her voice hard and mean, "why must you play with those Negroes in the schoolyard?"

"Those Negroes" were Effa's brothers and sisters. While Effa's skin was light, like her mother's, her siblings were dark, like their father. People with dark skin couldn't eat in certain restaurants or swim in public pools. Now it seemed they couldn't play with their sister, either.

"That's just the way things are," people said.

But it never made sense to Effa.

As Effa grew up in Philadelphia in the early 1900s, America grew up too. Bold new music—jazz—blared and folks stepped out in strange new shoes called sneakers.

After high school, Effa moved to New York City, which seemed like the perfect place to live the big life she dreamed of. Everyone there—everyone!—was talking about Babe Ruth, the Yankees' new slugging sensation. Effa went to games just to see his mighty swing.

Nothing prepared her for the crackling energy of the 1932 World Series at Yankee Stadium. New York was beating the Chicago Cubs, and the crowd roared its approval. In that swirl of excitement, Effa met a kind, fun-loving man, Abe Manley. Abe adored baseball.

He soon adored Effa, too. He would take Effa out on the town in Harlem, a bustling black neighborhood in New York City.

But something in Harlem really bothered Effa.

Even in black communities, most businesses were owned by white people. And black people were not hired for most jobs.

"That's just the way things are," people said.

But Effa knew it wasn't right.

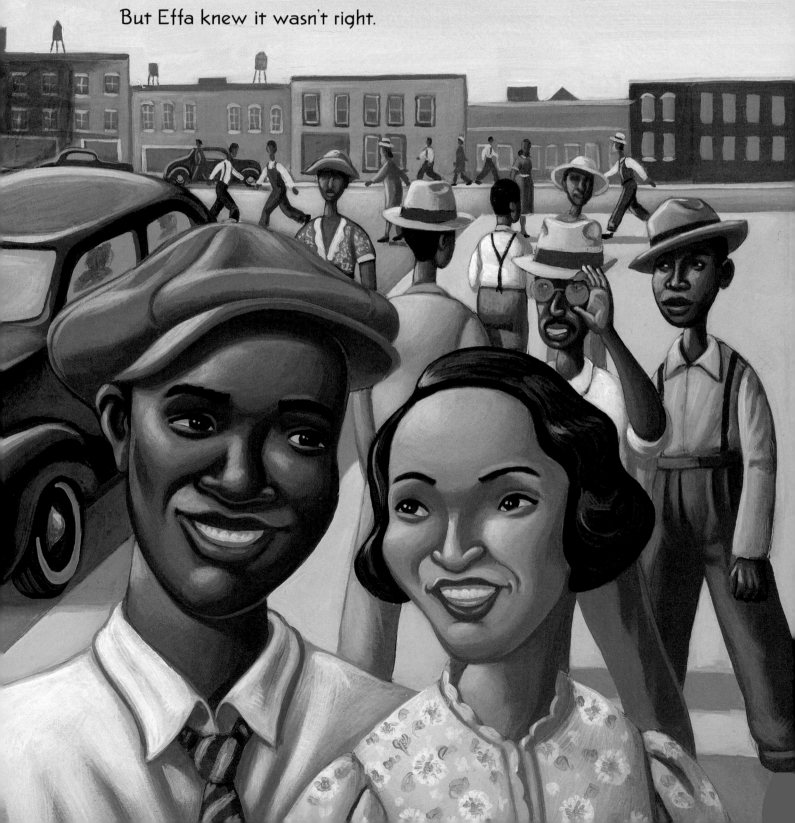

She organized the Citizens' League for Fair Play, a
group of community leaders. They urged Harlem's largest
department store to hire black salesclerks. The owner
said no.

Nobody believed a group of black people could change
a white businessman's mind, but the league fought anyway.
For weeks they marched in the street, carrying signs that said
"Don't Buy Where You Can't Work!"

They convinced their neighbors to shop elsewhere.

The store lost money.

But still, no black salesclerks.

The league kept marching.

Finally, they won. Newspapers reported the boycott's success. Effa proudly placed the articles in her scrapbook.

Before long, hundreds of black people were working in stores throughout Harlem.

The world of baseball was headed for change, too.

Abe and Effa married in 1935 and started a team, the Brooklyn Eagles, in the new Negro National League that Abe had helped establish.

Abe took the team south for spring training. But there was much to do in Brooklyn—organizing schedules, ordering

equipment, arranging transportation. Effa had never done work like that before, but the more she did, the more she enjoyed it. By the time the Eagles moved to New Jersey in 1936, Effa was handling almost all the team's business.

The city of Newark welcomed the Eagles. There was nothing more thrilling than a ball game at Ruppert Field: the hot, sweet-and-salty summer smells; the crack of the bat; people in their finest clothes standing, a few at first, willing the ball to keep going; then everyone at once; the thunderous cheer—the roar echoing blocks away.

When first baseman Mule Suttles came to bat, the crowd chanted, "Kick, Mule!" hoping to see his high-stepping home-run swing.

"Monte Irvin had one of the most magnificent arms that's ever been in baseball," Effa said. He was also an amazing shortstop. Irvin and power-hitting second baseman Larry Doby were one of the best double-play combinations ever.

Then there was Leon Day. "He played every place on the field except catcher," Effa said. "I don't mean he filled in. He *played* them." In broiling summer heat, Day would pitch the first game of a doubleheader, then trot out to play outfield for the second.

When Effa attended league meetings, other owners protested, "Baseball's no place for a woman." But over time, they came to respect her because she understood business, and she understood baseball.

Many owners only wanted to make money from their teams. But Effa cared about hers. She bought the best uniforms and a fancy, comfortable bus. She encouraged players to be active in the community and found them off-season jobs playing ball in Puerto Rico. Her players called her their "mother hen."

The Eagles had talent and skill. But for years, they were only second best. There was no beating the Kansas City Monarchs.

In 1946, they got their chance. It all came down to one final Negro League World Series game.

The best view was from the press box, but Effa sat in the stands, where the seats vibrated from foot-stomping excitement. Newark had a one-run lead going into the final inning. With two outs, the Monarchs had two men on base. Effa couldn't watch. She heard the crushing *thwack* of bat hitting ball and waited one awful second. Was it—say it wasn't!—a home run? The Newark crowd was cheering. Effa peeked through her fingers. The first baseman had made the catch! The Eagles were world champions! It was Effa's proudest moment.

The next year, Jackie Robinson joined the Brooklyn Dodgers—the first black player in the major leagues. So many people—not just baseball fans—were proud and hopeful about change and equality in America. Many black Americans became Dodgers fans that year.

Unfortunately, this meant the Negro Leagues lost fans and also started losing their best players—without even getting paid for them.

Some major league owners didn't know Negro League players had contracts; others didn't care. When Branch Rickey, general manager of the Brooklyn Dodgers, signed Don Newcombe in 1945, the Eagles lost an important player and received nothing in return.

Effa was glad to see her players get their big break, but she believed all teams—not just white ones—should be paid for their players.

She talked to the press and made people think about how unfair it was. Instead of saying, "That's just the way things are," some began to ask, "But why?"

So when Cleveland Indians owner Bill Veeck became interested in Larry Doby, he was ready to negotiate. In July 1947, he paid the Eagles $15,000, and Doby became the first black player in the American League.

Effa was losing another great player, but she wished him well. She told him, "Doby, keep hitting the ball out of the park."

He did.

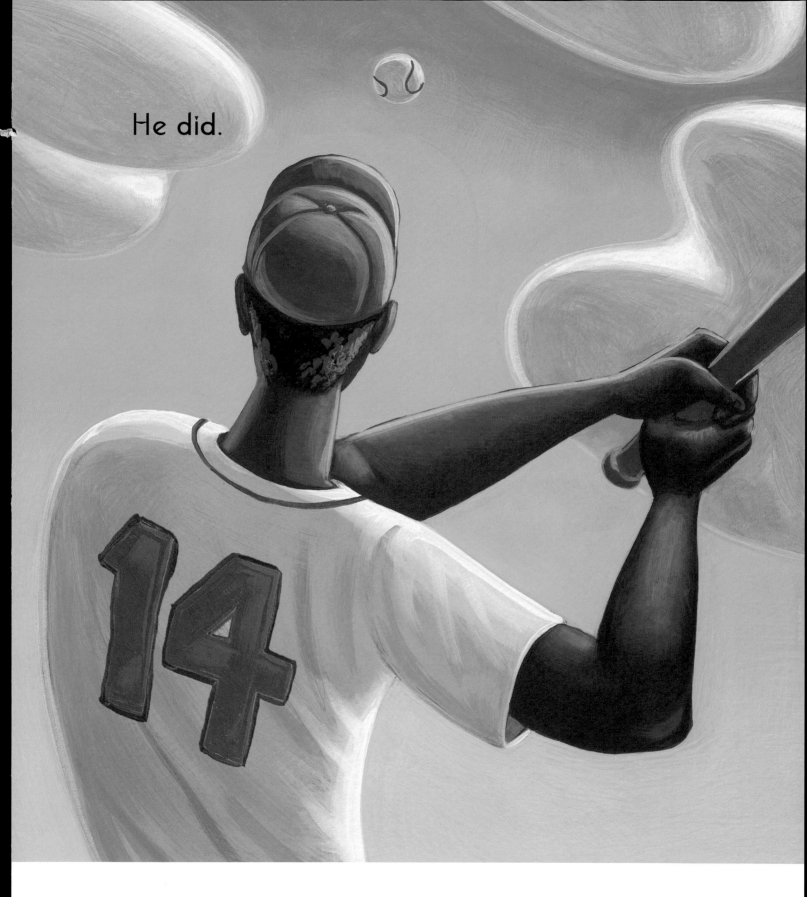

After that, the major league team owners always paid
Negro League teams for their players. But more and more
players left, and soon Negro League ball came to an end.

In 1952, Abe became ill and died. Effa lost her best friend, business partner, and truest love all at once. She often looked at her scrapbook to remind her of good times.

As she browsed those pages, something kept nagging at her. The history of the Negro Leagues was slipping away.

"That's just the way things are," people said.

But it broke Effa's heart.

In the 1970s she began a letter-writing campaign to convince the National Baseball Hall of Fame to acknowledge the best Negro League players. The hall had honored some who had also played in the majors, such as Jackie Robinson in 1962, but none who had played their entire career in the Negro Leagues.

When the hall appointed a committee to consider honoring Negro League stars, Effa was thrilled.

Between 1971 and 1977, the committee voted to induct nine Negro League players, including former Eagles star Monte Irvin. Then it announced it had completed its work.

Effa was outraged. She could name dozens more who deserved the honor, especially two Eagles—slugger Mule Suttles and Biz Mackey, who had managed the 1946 championship team.

She continued writing to the hall until she died in 1981.

The hall wasn't finished with Negro League players after all. Over the years, more of Effa's favorites were inducted. But many, including Suttles and Mackey, were not.

It wasn't right. It was just the way things were . . . until 2006.

On July 30, Suttles and Mackey—and ten other Negro League players—were finally inducted into the Hall of Fame. Effa would have been so proud.

Something else happened that day—something amazing. Effa was inducted along with them! In baseball's long history, Effa Manley was the first woman ever to be so honored.

She was recognized for all she did for her players, for her civil rights work, and for getting the major leagues to treat Negro League teams with respect.

On Effa's gravestone it says: SHE LOVED BASEBALL.

In 2006, baseball proved it loved her back.